Praise for Unlocked ... Joy:
Forgiveness Is the Key

"Melanie Shull is committed to the Word of God and the life-changing truth it brings to the hearts of men and women alike. Having led and written Bible studies for years while serving in ministry and having learned for herself the power of forgiveness from her own story, Melanie can be trusted to deliver the message God has given to her."

—Denise Hildreth Jones, founder of Reclaiming Hearts Ministries
Author of the *Savannah from Savannah* series,
The First Gardener, Secrets over Sweet Tea, and Hurricanes in Paradise

"Melanie Shull has to be one of the most radiantly contagious people I know. Her joy comes from her own deep-rooted pain set free by the forgiveness given and received in Christ Jesus. This hard-to-put-down read will unlock your heart because God wants you to be liberated too."

—Dr. Don Wilton, senior pastor of First Baptist Spartanburg, SC
Author and president of The Encouraging Word television ministry

"This is the Bible study you've been looking for. The theme of forgiveness is intricately woven into each chapter through Melanie Shull's own story and through needy, desperate, or imperfect Bible characters who came face to face with truth. You'll find an emphasis on getting answers from God's Word, and you'll discover how to make choices based on biblical wisdom. You can read this book on your own, but I encourage you to invite a group of friends to join you in a Bible study that will produce spiritual growth and deepened friendships. I highly recommend it."

—Carol Kent, director of the Speak Up Conference
Author of *He Holds My Hand: Experiencing God's Presence and Protection*

"Do you carry hidden scars and secret questions concerning your own life circumstances? Have you longed for freedom from destructive emotions that prevent you from moving forward into all God has for you? As Melanie Shull's faith journey unfolds, so do a myriad of biblical stories illustrating the power of forgiveness and God's sovereignty. *Unlocked Hearts, Unleashed Joy—Forgiveness Is the Key* is that rare combination of memoir and Bible study that allows the reader immediately to apply biblical teaching to their current struggles. If you are eager to live a more authentic, grace-filled life, Shull offers the tools to bravely take hold of all God's promises."

—Lucinda Secrest McDowell, author of *Ordinary Graces*

"According to Paul's words in Colossians 3:13, we are most like God when we forgive others of their sins against us. Regardless of the offense, unconditional forgiveness cancels the curse of hatred Satan uses to destroy us and opens our hearts as channels of God's love so God can find ways to use us. Such is the compelling testimony of Melanie Shull, now expressed in her Bible study *Unlocked Hearts, Unleashed Joy.* Those who choose to follow her Scripture-based steps to reconciliation will find real joy."

—Dr. Wayne J. Edwards, pastor, Heritage Baptist Church, Perry, GA
Director of Mature Ministries—Nicaragua Missions
Author of *Raising the Standard—One Pastor's Plea for a Return of Righteousness to the Church* and *Silent No More—the Ten Issues Christians Must No Longer Be Silent About*

"*Unlocked Hearts, Unleashed Joy—Forgiveness Is the Key* is a perfect picture of what God does when we allow Him to heal our wounds. If you struggle with wounds from the past, I encourage you to pick up this book and prepare to have a miraculous encounter with the God of grace. Melanie's story will encourage you and help you know you aren't alone. But even more, you'll see that not only can God heal you, but He can bring you to a place of joy you never imagined."

—Dr. Eddie Coakley, senior pastor, Trinity Baptist Church, Cayce, SC

UNLOCKED HEARTS, UNLEASHED JOY

Forgiveness Is the Key

To Cheryl,
May Christ unleash
His joy in your heart!
Melanie
Ps. 16:11

UNLOCKED HEARTS, UNLEASHED JOY

*Forgiveness
Is the Key*

MELANIE SHULL

Published by Redemption Press, PO Box 427, Enumclaw, WA 98022
Toll Free (844) 2REDEEM (273-3336)

Redemption Press is honored to present this title in partnership with the author. The views expressed or implied in this work are those of the author. Redemption Press provides our imprint seal representing design excellence, creative content and high quality production.

ISBN 13: 978-1-68314-773-2
Library of Congress Catalog Card Number: 2019935706

Table of Contents

About the Author

Melanie Shull believes in the power of story, especially the transforming power of God's story through grace and an ever-growing faith in Jesus Christ. Since 2009, as founder and editor in chief of *Living Real Magazine*, Melanie has provided a unique platform for ordinary Christ-followers to "show and tell" how real faith influences everyday life. She is also the founder of the Living Real Co-Ed Conference—bringing the magazine to life. A musician, writer, speaker, worship leader, and Bible study teacher, Melanie loves ushering people into the presence of Jesus Christ. From her heart flow worship, encouragement, hospitality, and a deep love for God and His Word.

Melanie's previously published works include a Bible study, *Renew, Refresh, Refine ~ Your Heart, Soul, and Mind* and *The Red Carpet Journal*, a resource for writing God's Word on your heart. Besides having a serious coffee-mug fetish, Melanie is a loud and proud football fan. She loves doing life with her husband, Rick, in a not-quite-yet empty nest in the middle of their university alma mater town of Columbia, South Carolina—Gamecock country. To contact Melanie or to find out more about *Living Real Magazine*, go to www.melanieshull.com or www.livingrealmag.com. Don't forget to follow Melanie on social media.

Facebook: @writermelanieshull and @LivingRealMag

Twitter: @melanieshull

Instagram: @melanieshullauthor

@LivingRealMag

Pinterest: @melanieshull

Preface

Hello, friend! You just made my heart smile. Not only did you pick up this study book, but you are also reading this letter—a letter I've poured my heart and soul into. You and I probably have some things in common. In fact, I wrote this book because I believe when we're transparent with our stories, we connect more easily with others who walk similar paths. You see, like so many, I know what it's like to live with deep wounds. But I've also learned to forgive in spite of those wounds. Forgiveness is the key that releases us from a past of pain and unleashes God's indescribable joy to flow freely within our souls.

That's what I want you to discover too.

Maybe you struggle with a stubborn heart that doesn't want to let go of the past. Maybe you need encouragement and answers for yourself or someone else. Or maybe you long to meet someone who understands what you're going through. Whatever the case, I know what it's like to strive in silence, to hide in guilt and shame, and to feel alone.

I believe every person experiences a locked-up heart. An unbeliever's imprisoned heart is the result of unbelief and unconfessed sin. The same is true for a believer.

So what's the difference?

The door to the unbeliever's heart has not yet been unlocked. This keeps them imprisoned, along with their cellmates: sin, guilt, shame, regret, and the like. The keeper of the keys, Jesus Christ, stands outside the cellblock, constantly calling to unbelievers to let Him set their hearts free. If by faith they will confess Him as Lord, trust Him with their lives, and follow Him wholeheartedly, then His cross-shaped key will unlock their hearts and set them free.

However, Jesus has already unlocked the door to the believer's heart, using the key of forgiveness by grace through faith (Ephesians 2:8–9). He set us free from the bondage of sin and gave us power through the Holy Spirit to live victoriously over sin.

Sometimes, though, we choose to live as if we're still imprisoned. Whether or not we intend to ignore our unconfessed sins, those sins can slam shut the door of our hearts, locking in cellmates like fear, bitterness, anger—even hate. When left to grow unchecked and unchallenged, these sins strain our relationship with our heavenly Father, hinder our effectiveness for Christ, and affect our relationships with others. It's a miserable existence.

Some believers sentence themselves to years, even life, with a locked-up heart. They carry around regret, shame, and guilt like a prison ball and chain. I know. I walked around in shackles for many years, but I couldn't figure out what held me back. The good news is that God never stops pursuing us, longing to unlock the areas of our hearts we've allowed to slam shut.

As believers, we cannot let down our guards but must tend to our relationship with our heavenly Father daily. We need to guard our hearts above all else (Proverbs 4:23) because from our hearts flows the essence of who we are. Guarding our hearts against the debris of sin will allow joy to flow freely and help us maintain our influence for Christ.

Throughout this Bible study, we'll look into several scriptural accounts of those who've encountered God's pursuit of their hearts. Through the counsel of the Word and being honest with the Lord, you may discover Him pursuing you as well. Invite the Holy Spirit to examine your heart. Allow Him to teach you and to identify any culprits that prevent God's joy from flowing uninhibited through you. We have access to the key to freedom and joy, but we must use that key if we are to experience abundant life through Christ Jesus.

Are you ready? Let's do this.

By His Grace Alone,

Melanie

"No one enters into the real joy of the Lord in spite of the hard times, but squarely through the hard times."

~ Ann Voskamp

Introduction

Revenge, the ABC nighttime television series that debuted in 2011, intrigued me and immediately sucked me in. I didn't want to miss a single episode in real time. The main character, a woman in her twenties, believed a certain family was responsible for her father's murder during her childhood. From the devastating moment of discovering what she believed to be the truth about her father's death she became obsessed with planning her revenge and retaliation.

I couldn't help rooting for her to succeed. She didn't just want to get even—she was out for blood. She desired destruction of a family who'd built their success on dirty business dealings, corrupt politics, and other scandalous deeds. I wanted her to get her revenge.

However, as the series went on, my feelings changed. Even though the story was fictitious, my infatuation with the show bothered me. Taking revenge on the people who'd pierced the character's heart did nothing to heal it. Instead, her thirst for revenge caused more devastation. All her scheming simply brought more pain, which kept her from moving on. With each takedown, she craved more destruction. This woman's obsession with revenge not only became her life, but it also formed a noose, slowly tightening around her neck and ultimately suffocating her. Her life became a pitiful existence.

Through this fictional television series, God reminded me why He said, "Vengeance is mine, I will repay" (Romans 12:19 ESV).

The same revenge-filled attitude sweeps across our nation today in real life, like the California wildfires that consumed whatever lay in their path. Revenge! The popular mantra "You will pay, no matter what it costs" speaks volumes about the spiritual condition of many wounded hearts.

Instead of fighting hard for healing, many people put on boxing gloves and look for the perfect moment to deliver a knockout punch. The scenarios play out in the media every day—the takedown of teachers, pastors, celebrities, politicians, journalists, judges, and more. The mindset of revenge is not only prevalent in the secular culture but has also crept into the hearts of Christians.

The purpose of this study is not to condone criminal acts or to vindicate the individuals who've harmed us. Rather, I wrote this book to help us surrender ourselves and our wounds to the Savior, who wants to transform our suffering into something beautiful for His glory and our good.

Left to their own devices, fear and anger grow into bitterness and hate. They root in the soil of our hearts, where joy should flourish. The prayer Jesus taught His disciples, "Forgive us our debts, as we also have forgiven our debtors" (Matthew 6:12 ESV), remains relevant today. You and I must practice the holy art of forgiveness.

Developing a forgiving spirit is not a sign of weakness or a willingness to give up. Forgiveness is about love, courage, and strength. It's about breaking the stronghold of evil on our hearts. A forgiving spirit refuses to allow the one who harmed us to keep their control over our thoughts and minds. If we don't cultivate a forgiving spirit, a bitter spirit will choke the life out of us. As Christ has forgiven us, we must also forgive. We cannot love if we harbor hate against another human being. We cannot move forward until we develop peace with what lies behind.

The encounter I'm about to share with you begins with a secret—one I kept locked inside for years. This secret could have destroyed me, and revenge didn't set my heart free. The key of forgiveness did. When my secret pain surfaced, that pain drew me tighter into my Father's arms. Through His tender compassion and the Comforter's wise counsel, I stepped into a lifelong journey of unlocking and unleashing the joy of Jesus in my life.

Throughout these eight lessons, you'll discover that the enemy didn't turn out to be who I thought it was. In fact, I had locked the door to my heart from the inside.

I'm praying for you to commit before the Lord to fight the right enemy, in the right way, with the right key. I promise—it's more than worth it!

"The enemy may think he can wear you down without much of a fight, but wait until he encounters the fight of God's Spirit in you. Because...This. Means. War."

~ Priscilla Shirer

LESSON 1

The Nightmare

My heart pounds until it might burst from my chest.
Fear locks in hard and fast. It's him! He's at the front door!

Home alone, holding my sweet baby boy, I try to shake off the cold hand
of terror gripping my throat. Trembling, I somehow make it into the foyer.
With sweaty palms, I slowly turn the knob, cracking open the door.

Standing on the stoop just inches away, he glares at me.
"If you ever tell, I will come back and take your baby."

The nightmare ends as I jolt awake. I sit straight up in bed, shaken and frozen in fear. With tears streaming, I can barely breathe. I gather my emotions enough to ease out from under the covers, trying not to wake my husband. I tiptoe into the bathroom to wipe away the tears—again.

Why do I have this recurring nightmare? Why can't I share it with my husband? Why is it coming back now?

***

I was twenty-six, happily married, and thrilled to be a mom. At the time, I didn't realize I'd locked my heart sometime between the ages of thirteen and fourteen.

A leader in my home church, a dear family friend, began paying attention to me. Young and naïve, I thought this was normal. I should have been able to trust him. However, his inappropriate behavior soon popped that bubble.

One evening at a church event, this attention turned into an invasion of my innocence. Later, I knew what had occurred was wrong. This violation of personal space, this sexual misconduct, caused confusion in my young heart and impressionable mind. I struggled to process it all. That night, I chose to confide in one close friend, but I wouldn't mention this moment again for years.

My secret.

My wound.

For fourteen years, I believed the old adage "Out of sight, out of mind." I didn't speak about the incident, so I thought it had gone away. Since my perpetrator had also left South Carolina, no one would ever know.

Then one day, someone mentioned he was back in town. This news triggered my nightmare. I hadn't realized the severity of my wound until the pain came rushing back. My heart had locked up, and I discovered I was chained to some not-so-friendly cellmates.

***

We all have or will experience a wounded heart. To understand a wounded heart, Google the word "wound." Write what you find.

Wound means:

_____

_____

_____

_____

_____

_____

According to Strong's Hebrew Lexicon search (http://www.eliyah.com/lexicon.html) the Hebrew word for "wound" is makkah or makkeh, meaning a blow, wound, slaughter. Hebrew is much richer than our English language. A blow to the heart, or a slaughtering of the heart, gives a more graphic picture than the word "wound."

Read Isaiah 53.

How was Jesus wounded for us? Write down the descriptive words or phrases you find.

_____

_____

_____

_____

_____

Wounds come in all shapes and sizes, thrust upon us in all sorts of ways. Some leave scars for life. Others fade away with time. Scars are physical reminders of past pain, and each one tells a story.

For years, I had a three- to four-inch scar on the inside of my left thigh. The scar has since faded, but my memory of the story behind it hasn't. I was in ninth or tenth grade—old enough to be home alone. My parents had asked me to pick up some tree limbs and debris in our backyard, so I headed outside to do the work.

When I picked up a short log, I didn't know it had a stick attached. That stick gashed the inside of my thigh.

I don't deal well with blood. I've never passed out, but I've come close. This was one of those times. With no one around to help, I headed into the house to lie down. But first, I had to clean the wound.

Ugghh!

By the time my mom returned home, I was lying on the couch, wound cleaned and bandaged, a cold washcloth draped across my forehead. I didn't attempt any more yard work that day.

Depending on the severity of a wound, it may need professional attention or even stitches. Thank goodness mine was not that serious. However, we must clean and bandage our wounds to reduce the risk of infection.

A wounded heart is no different. If we don't treat it immediately, infection can set in without our knowledge. My nightmares proved I had not tended to the wounds my sexual predator had caused. The wound had become infected.

What's the story behind your wounded heart? Did you suffer rejection, verbal abuse, or bullying? Maybe your wounded heart came through physical, emotional, or sexual abuse. Family, friends, co-workers, bosses, enemies, even church members can wound us deeply. Everyone we meet has the potential to hurt us. Depending on our response to those wounds, one of two things will happen. Either God will lovingly use them to make us better, or the enemy will exploit them to make us bitter. Without realizing it, I had allowed the enemy to take advantage of my pain.

***

Read Genesis 27:41–31:55.

Jacob loved Rachel from the moment he saw her. Rachel's father, Laban, promised to give her to Jacob as his bride, but only if he worked for him for seven years. Because Jacob loved Rachel with all his heart, he agreed. However, Laban wanted to remain faithful to the custom of his people, so he needed his older daughter, Leah, to marry first. So he tricked Jacob.

Leah followed Jacob into the dark marriage tent. Thinking Leah was Rachel, he consummated the marriage. What gut-wrenching pain he must have felt when he realized Laban had deceived him. Then Laban required seven more years of work in exchange for Rachel.

Talk about a nightmare. I can't imagine waking up next to a stranger instead of the man I thought I'd married the night before. But I'm sure it would make me more than angry and bitter. I'm not sure I would have been as gracious as Jacob. I probably would have packed my bags, loaded up my camel, and gone home.

However, Jacob remembered God's promise.

Re-read Genesis 28:13–15.

God had made a promise Jacob could cling to. Jacob believed God would take care of him and multiply his children.

Read on through verse 22.

What did Jacob do in response?

_____

_____

_____

_____

_____

_____

_____

_____

As Jacob remained in Haran, he clung to that promise and to the joy of knowing he lived in the presence of God. Not only did God take care of Jacob and his broken heart, but He also blessed everything he touched, making him a wealthy man. By the time Jacob had completed his second seven years in Haran, God had supplied him with everything he needed to move forward and finish His redemption story. Now Jacob could pack up all God had blessed him with, load up his camel train, and head back to Canaan, his homeland.

The Lord had devised a plan for Jacob, Leah, and Rachel even before the creation of the world. Through miraculous events and despite a dysfunctional family tree, God honored His promise. From Jacob's seed, the twelve tribes of Israel were born.

***

Let's examine Jacob's story a little further. Take your time and look for nuggets of truth you may not have seen before.

Describe how you felt about Jacob's response to Laban's trickery.

_____

_____

_____

Once Jacob married Rachel, why didn't peace and harmony fill their home?

_____

_____

_____

How many years did Jacob end up serving Laban before he went back to Canaan?

_____

Describe how God's faithfulness to Jacob brings you comfort in your current situation. If it doesn't, describe why not.

_____

_____

_____

_____

If you have lived through nightmarish circumstances, describe how you responded to the situation.

_____

_____

_____

_____

_____

***

Life isn't all unicorns and confetti. Everyone has times of celebration, times of weeping, and times of healing. King Solomon reminds us there is a season for everything.

Read Ecclesiastes 3:1–8.

What seasons of life are listed in this passage?

_____

_____

_____

_____

_____

Between 2014 and 2017, my family dealt with much grief. We lost seven close friends and family members to cancer, rapidly progressing Alzheimer's, and other ailments. The most tragic was McKinsey, our daughter's best friend since third grade, who died instantly in a single-car crash at the age of twenty.

This season of sorrow exhausted us. We could barely overcome the initial shock and pain of losing one person before receiving another call about someone else. Through it all, I witnessed God's grace as His strength carried us.

When McKinsey died, my daughter and her friends rallied around each other in search of answers and comfort. The love they showed one another was priceless. Through the grace of God, they even helped McKinsey's mom through the grieving process. They stepped in to be "sisters" to McKinsey's only brother, "Little David," and haven't stopped caring for McKinsey's family to this day. God used McKinsey's death to draw her mom to Himself in ways that still amaze us.

This grieving mother formed the McKinsey Foundation because of her daughter's love for the orphans she had fallen in love with on a mission trip to Uganda. Many of these children had no hope of an education. Today, because of the McKinsey Foundation, over one hundred students now attend school, fully supported, and hear about Jesus.

We told McKinsey's story in our 2015 Spring issue of *Living Real Magazine*. Even though she had surrendered her life to Christ only two years prior to her death, McKinsey left a powerful legacy that continues to shine for Jesus.

I also saw God's power, strength, and grace fill my husband as he tenderly cared for his mother, an Alzheimer's victim, during the last forty days of her life. God's strength sustained him, and His grace was sufficient to see my husband and our family through those strenuous days of uncertainty.

God's grace and mercy kept us again in the weeks prior to the passing of our cousin Robby, who died of cancer. His grandmother had passed away a few months before. Sick and in poor health for several years, she had asked the Lord not to allow her to outlive her grandson. She had already buried her husband and stepson after a plane crash many years earlier, and she couldn't bear to lay Robby to rest too. Her faith was strong, but her emotional state waned. God honored her request. She died first and, along with loved ones who had gone before, she surely greeted her grandson at his arrival at his eternal destination, in the glorious presence of Jesus Christ.

I could share many more similar stories, all with the same conclusion. Our time on earth is brief, and Christ wants us to live well, fully engaged in the joy of His presence.

Maybe you're in a season of deep wounds, hurt, rejection, or abuse, and your life feels like a nightmare. Maybe you're in a season of deep grief, feeling lost and shuffling through the day with no direction or purpose. Or maybe you're in a season of discovery, learning to identify the hand of God in your life. Whatever season you're in, I promise it will change.

The good news is that God never changes. His essence dictates that He remain the same yesterday, today, and forevermore (Hebrews 13:8). He is our immovable Rock in whom our strength lies. He is our faithful Redeemer, always working to restore everything that's broken. God makes all things beautiful in His time. He tirelessly crafts your brokenness and mine into something eternally stunning. He promises to complete the amazing work He has begun in all who believe (Philippians 1:6).

Remember this: the God of Abraham, Isaac, and Jacob is also your God. Run to Him with arms outstretched. Lay your requests at His feet. He's listening to your cry for help. He will cuddle up with you as He catches every tear. He's reaching for you and will carry you through.

 He will cover you with his feathers; you will take refuge under his wings. His faithfulness will be a protective shield. (Psalm 91:4)

In the space provided, describe the season you're in. List some ways you see God's faithfulness.

_____

_____

_____

_____

_____

_____

_____

_____

The following prayer is for anyone to pray when they're in a hard place. If you're not in the midst of a difficult season, write a prayer of your own in the journal space provided.

> *Dear Lord,* I know You can hear me. I know You're there. Please give me a stronger faith to believe You will never leave me. Please help me to see Your faithfulness as You walk beside me through this season of pain. My heart hurts, Lord, and You know why. As You did for Jacob, please give me strength to respond to my wound with love and grace rather than anger and bitterness. Help me to remember Your promises, to lean in to You more. Then when this season is over, I can walk out on the other side, stronger and better than before. In the name of Jesus. Amen.

_____

_____

_____

_____

_____

_____

_____

_____

_____

_____

_____

_____

_____

_____

_____

_____

"The Lord is my light and my salvation;
Whom shall I fear? The Lord is the strength
of my life; Of whom shall I be afraid?

Psalm 27:1 NKJV

LESSON 2

Secluded but Never Alone

"Your little family doesn't need you, especially like this," the enemy whispered in my ear. "You're doing them no good. Walk out the door and never come back. They'll be better off without you."

The enemy bombarded my mind with lies, leaving me confused and depressed, alone in my despair.

***

When I was around five years old, I was on *The Mr. Knozit Show*, a local Saturday morning television show for kids. The host, Mr. Knozit, always asked the kids, "What do you want to be when you grow up?"

When it was my turn to answer, I didn't hesitate. I blurted out, "A mommy!"

Unlike most girls my age, I didn't want to be a teacher, a nurse, or even a movie star. Even though I had been singing and playing the piano since age three, my heart's desire wasn't to sing on Broadway or perform at Carnegie Hall. I wanted to be a mom.

Twenty years later, and after five years of marriage, God honored this little girl's simple dream. On September 26, 1989, I became a mom to a son weighing eight pounds, seven ounces. I didn't realize it at the time, but Jesus would anchor my soul through the storm that arrived shortly after the birth of our first baby.

When the recurring nightmare began, my baby was nine months old. In the solace of home, while still adjusting to being a new mom, I began to shut down. I refused to tell anyone about the nightmare or the dark place I was sinking into. The only person I told was Jesus.

My Savior.

My best friend.

My spiritual heart was in code mode. I didn't understand what was going on. My heart desperately needed reviving, and Jesus knew it. He was there. Every moment. Every day. Every night. Though I felt trapped, He never abandoned me. God knew this piece of my story before the beginning of time, and He used this pain to draw me to Himself. I was in the right place to receive His miraculous work of heart.

Although I felt secluded in my pain, He never left me alone.

***

Remember God's promise to Jacob from lesson 1? God promised to take care of Jacob and multiply his offspring. Jacob fathered the twelve tribes of Israel. (God later changed Jacob's name to Israel. See Genesis 32:28). Joseph was Jacob's eleventh son.

Joseph had a special place in his father's heart because he was the offspring of the true love between his father, Jacob, and his mother, Rachel.

One day, Joseph found himself trapped, secluded, and alone. But was he really alone?

Read Genesis 37.

What stands out to you about Joseph's situation?

_____

_____

_____

_____

_____

Why did Joseph's brothers plot to get rid of him?

_____

_____

_____

_____

_____

Even though he didn't know how his situation would change over time, Joseph was right where God wanted him to be—secluded but not alone. God needed his undivided attention so He could fulfill His purposes for Joseph. This piece of Joseph's story shows us a pivotal moment in Joseph's heart.

I'm sure fear gripped Joseph and he thought all was lost. After all, he was trapped at the bottom of a pit. But he wasn't alone. God was working, and His good plan did not include leaving Joseph hopeless in a trap.

Who pulled Joseph out of the pit?

_____

_____

Have you ever felt trapped in a place of despair, without hope? If so, describe your situation:

_____

_____

_____

_____

The Midianite traders took Joseph to Egypt, where all of Israel would eventually become enslaved and remain so for 400 years. Even though his brothers had sold him as a slave, Joseph was never alone, although it seemed so.

***

When I was twenty-six, my life became blurred with fear. The recurring nightmare always took me to a scary place that crushed my joy. But God used this pit of despair to draw me to Himself. Although I felt alienated from everyone around me, I was never alone. God moved me in closer, so the Holy Spirit could teach me the difference between His counsel of truth and the enemy's lies.

This is one of the hardest lessons for believers, but you can learn it as we move through this study.

Satan has only one plan for every person—to steal, kill, and destroy. He works tirelessly, attempting to defeat us. He'll do anything to diminish our influence for God and His glory.

 The thief does not come except to steal, and to kill, and to destroy. I have come that they may have life, and that they may have it more abundantly. (John 10:10 NKJV)

God etched His perfect plan for us in His mind long before He began knitting us together in our mother's womb.

Read Psalm 139:1–6.

After examining these verses, describe how well God knows you. Be specific.

_____

_____

_____

_____

_____

_____

_____

According to verses 7–12, where can we hide from God?

_____

_____

_____

_____

_____

_____

_____

I always use verses 13–16 when telling my life's story. I like to frame these verses as my Scripture picture. You should too.

As you write verses 13–16, imagine yourself holding the Father's hand, speaking these words to Him.

_____

_____

_____

_____

_____

_____

***

My struggle didn't catch my Father off guard. He knew what He needed to do. He also knew how to heal my heart, restore my joy, and put me back together stronger than before. But first, I needed to clear my heart of all distractions. I had locked my heart into a prison cell crowded with uninvited cellmates, particularly fear of the dream. As I wrestled with fear, God commanded it to flee. While I cried out to Him for help, He corralled my other cellmates: bitterness, anger, and hate. The Lord surrounded my enemies and set me free.

 The angel of the Lord encamps around those who fear him, and delivers them. (Psalm 34:7 ESV)

As I wrote this Bible study, I discovered a spiritual warfare song by Michael W. Smith called "Surrounded (Fight My Battles)." In it, Michael tells us to exchange a spirit of heaviness for the garment of praise (Isaiah 61:3). Smith declares, "This is how we fight our battles."

When we lay down our hearts in surrender and lift our voices in praise, the spirit of heaviness falls away. The Lord of the heavenly armies fights our battles for us.

During the most frightening time of my life, Jesus pushed in closer to my fearful but faithful heart. He gave me space to question and a strong shoulder to cry on, all while securing me in His gentle embrace. Just as He didn't leave Joseph to die in the trap, He didn't leave me in my pit of despair.

And He won't leave you either.

 My sheep hear My voice, and I know them, and they follow Me. And I give them eternal life, and they shall never perish; neither shall anyone snatch them out of My hand. (John 10:27–28 NKJV)

I had some tear-filled counseling sessions with my Wonderful Counselor in my kitchen while my husband was at work. While I washed clothes, ironed, and folded, the enemy berated me. "You're not good enough." However, the Prince of Peace spoke truth into my soul, reminding me that I'm His child, and He's my God.

I prayed with raw honesty about my fear of my perpetrator showing up and taking my child. I laid this fear before the Lord. Soon I soon realized I couldn't keep my secret anymore. I had to tell somebody. I needed help, so He guided me to a man I trusted, who had discipled my husband and me during our dating years.

I made a phone call to our trusted friend and former college pastor. After I poured out my heart and secret to him, he gave me wise counsel, which led me to make another phone call—one that would change my life forever.

***

Before you go any further, spend some time putting on the garment of praise. Surrender your heavy heart before the Lord and let Him fight for you. Journal your thoughts of thanksgiving and praise in the space provided and let the Lord lift your heaviness.

"In the shadow of my hurt, forgiveness feels like a decision to reward my enemy. But in the shadow of the cross, forgiveness is merely a gift from one undeserving soul to another."

~ Andy Stanley

LESSON 3

An Unexpected Gift

Nervous as a rat in a trap, I dialed the number. When he answered, I drew a deep breath and forged ahead. "This is Melanie. I need to speak with you."

I took the first step and made the appointment.

***

Wow, this was happening. I was not having a nightmare. I had spoken with the one who'd stolen my childhood innocence, the one who'd filled my nights with fear. I'd made an appointment to meet him—and my fear—face to face.

My pastor had advised me not to meet with my perpetrator alone or in a secluded location. I knew I would be safe, not because other people worked nearby but because I trusted my Lord. I was confident He had gone before me, and I was willing to take this risk of faith.

That afternoon, I drove a short distance to a local church, where I would see my perpetrator for the first time in about seven years. I'm sure he wondered why I was coming. My phone call must have caught him off guard. Did he think I would press charges after all this time? Did he fear I wanted revenge? In his mind, he probably replayed his actions while he waited for me to arrive. He must have been nervous. Would he have regrets?

When I arrived, the setting wasn't what I expected. There was no paved parking lot. I had to park in a sand lot. His office was a small room, detached from the main church building. Here in South Carolina we call them portables. We use them as extra classrooms.

In this troubling setting, I got out of the car, opened the rear door. My hands shook as I lifted my son from his car seat, and my stomach knotted. But despite my anxiety, I knew I was obeying the Lord. I needed to do this, or my healing process wouldn't begin.

I stepped up to the office door and knocked, my palm sweaty. Footsteps sounded inside, and then he opened the door. My heart dropped into the deepest part of my knotted-up stomach.

Moments later, I sat across the desk from the man of my nightmare, the object of my fear.

My memory is a little fuzzy, but with tears streaming down my face, I managed to say something like this: "I've hated you for a long time, and I can't keep living like this. My anger and bitterness toward you are eating me alive. I came to ask you to forgive me for hating you."

I'll never forget the look on his face. He seemed stunned, like a bird that crashes into a window, knocks itself to the ground, and can't get up. At that moment, I couldn't believe any of this was happening. *Did I really ask for his forgiveness after all he's put me through? I need to get out of here. What was I thinking? What is he thinking?* My heart pounded so loudly, he surely heard it.

Then God broke through the intense wall of silence and calmed my thoughts.

"Yes, I forgive you, but you did nothing wrong," my perpetrator said, tears in his eyes. "This was all my fault, and I'm the one who needs forgiveness. Will you please forgive me?"

Now I was speechless. Whatever I'd expected, his repentant heart wasn't it. He seemed genuine, broken. Who knew the conversation would swerve in this direction? Who knew two hearts would encounter a cleansing that day? Who knew both hearts needed healing?

God.

He'd known it all along.

The all-knowing One knew how this would go down. Nothing surprises our Creator, because He wrote the story. I needed to meet my offender face to face. I thought the meeting's purpose was to begin my healing process, but God knew more needed to happen. He honored my obedience as I took a step of faith and asked my perpetrator's forgiveness. Then He allowed me to hear him ask for and receive forgiveness. Because I had trusted God wholeheartedly, I received an unexpected gift.

I never would have chosen to meet with the person in my nightmare. Initially, I thought I had nothing to be sorry for. However, when we deny self, we look more like Christ—the One who denied Himself to the death to offer us forgiveness. Taking up my cross and following Christ was a risk worth taking, even if my offender hadn't responded the way he had.

I cannot describe the river of freedom that rushed through my soul. As soon as I asked for forgiveness, I felt as if a key had been inserted into the cell door of my heart—the door I had slammed shut, locking out much of my joy for fourteen years. As the key turned, the door flew open wide. It did not hesitate. It did not creak on its hinges. It flew open unhindered, flooding my soul with joy once again.

Instead of pacing in a suffocating cell, I waltzed across the dance floor with my Prince of Peace.

I was free!

Our responses dictate whether we dance in freedom or pace in defeat. Forgiveness does not erase consequences but unclutters the heart. My obedience did not mean I would become friends with this person. My gift of forgiveness did not erase the past. Rather, the entire event gave me the freedom to move beyond my past.

 For whoever would save his life will lose it, but whoever loses his life for my sake will find it. (Matthew 16:25 ESV)

We need healthy boundaries, especially when abuse is involved. But my strategic action was the first step in unlocking my heart and reclaiming my joy. God surprised me with more than I ever could have hoped for or imagined (Ephesians 3:20).

An unexpected gift. What a good, good God we serve.

We all need to give and receive the key of forgiveness. Too many people harbor grudges and hate, waiting for the perfect moment to inflict pain on the one who has hurt them. But God hasn't called us to seek revenge. He reserves revenge for Himself. In His perfect time, He will serve holy justice. We are called to forgive as Christ has forgiven us, and to let go.

Offering forgiveness to my perpetrator was only my first lesson. I had to practice forgiveness over and over again in the years to come. I needed to continue to experience God restoring my relationship with Him and others and conforming my heart to Christ's heart. God had much more in store for my future—just as He did with Joseph.

***

Read Genesis 37:36 then chapters 39–44. As you read, make a list of the circumstances Joseph finds himself in, good and bad. I'll help get you started:

Joseph is sold into slavery.

_____

_____

_____

_____

_____

_____

_____

_____

Read Genesis 45:1–14. This portion of the story sheds light on God's purpose for Joseph's suffering.

Why do you think God allowed all that happened to Joseph in Egypt?

_____

_____

_____

_____

_____

_____

_____

What event made Joseph realize it was time to reveal his identity to his brothers?

_____

_____

_____

_____

How did Joseph's brothers respond to his revelation?

_____

_____

_____

_____

Why is forgiveness vital to our joy in Christ?

_____

_____

_____

_____

Can you think of someone who needs your forgiveness—the key to unlocking your heart and theirs? If so, write out a prayer. Let the Spirit search your heart. Be honest and confess whatever sin He brings to your mind. Recognize that your unforgiveness suffocates your joy. Trust Him to unlock your heart and unleash that joy. Tell Him you're willing to do whatever it takes to heal your heart. It's hard, but it's worth it.

It is for your benefit in the presence of Christ, so that we may not be taken advantage of by Satan. For we are not ignorant of his schemes. (2 Corinthians 2:10–11)

If God has unlocked your heart through the power of forgiveness, journal your story on the journal pages provided. Then write a prayer of thanksgiving to God. Ask Him for the courage to share your story with someone, maybe during your small-group time. Also ask Him to show you who to tell and when to tell them what God has done in your life.

"Though I did not grow under my mother's heart, God placed me in her heart before the world began."

~ Melanie Shull

LESSON 4

The Loving Option: Adoption

Fifty-seven days. That's how long I was in foster care.

I was almost six months old when my forever parents walked into the room. I'm told I flashed a big, toothless grin, reached out my chubby little arms, and wrapped them tight around the neck of the man who would soon be my daddy. That's when the lady in charge said she would leave the three of us alone for about thirty minutes. (In the 1960s, when a couple met a prospective child for adoption, the prospective parents were often left alone with the child to determine whether or not this was the right child for them.) Thirty minutes didn't seem long enough to make a life-changing decision. But my forever daddy didn't need even that much time.

"Ma'am, you don't have to go anywhere. We're not leaving without her."

I'm told my daddy said those words without hesitation, not needing thirty minutes to make up their minds. They had chosen me, and I was going home. As my mom used to say, "Melanie hasn't let go of her daddy's neck since."

Adoption is a beautiful gift wrapped in grace—a gift both received and given. The adoptive parents' lives are richer, and the child receives joy—a connection with a family for a lifetime. Parents need a heart of compassion in order to bring a child into a family. Adopting requires sacrifice, unconditional love, and a steady stream of patience, wisdom, and strength. To immerse a child into a family rhythm, the entire family must compose a new song together. Where love, acceptance, and grace are reciprocal, the family will thrive, even through the storms of life.

Our family always celebrated adoptions. I gained a sister, Michelle, through adoption two years later. Though our parents are no longer here to celebrate with us, we still enjoy getting together on our adopted days. Mine is March twenty-seventh, and my sister's is May fifth.

Knowing I was adopted made me feel special. I don't remember anything about the day my parents adopted me—I was only five and a half months old—so I've always loved to watch our home movies of that event.

Captured on film is the homemade flag my mother made from a cloth diaper. She attached that flag to our front yard light post, announcing, "It's a girl!" In the film, you can also see everyone who visited our house that evening to congratulate my parents and meet me. My parents say over one hundred people dropped by that evening. Each time someone came in to pick me up from my crib, I flashed that huge, toothless grin.

My parents were told one tidbit of information about my background: I came from a musical family. They should be on the lookout, they were told, for musical talent that might emerge early. When I was three, my daddy bought a piano. He said he'd always wanted to learn to play, so he began taking lessons. I climbed up on the piano stool every day and pounded out tunes I already knew, like "Jesus Loves Me."

Because I played by ear at such a young age, my mother decided I should begin piano lessons the summer after the first grade. From age six through my freshman year in college, I took lessons. Oh, and my dad quit his lessons after six months. He said he didn't have the time. I think he bought the piano only to stir up my gift.

My daddy didn't let our gender stop him from teaching my sister and me about the finer things in life, like football. I fell in love with the sport. By the time I was five years old, I knew all the referee hand signals for the game. My father and I watched hours of football together, ran around in the yard throwing the football during halftimes, and I even stood on the sidelines at the high school games when my dad ran the chains on occasion. When it came time to choose teams to cheer for, he always gave me first dibs. My team won most of the time. My scientific strategy? I chose the team based on whether I liked the color of their uniforms. To this day, I always think about my dad when I watch a game.

Many adopted children want to know why they were given up. But the question never bothered me. I owned being adopted right from the start. Why wouldn't I? My parents never hid the truth, and they always celebrated God's design for us as a family.

Some of my fondest memories include vacations at the lake. Our family owned a small weekend home on Lake Murray in South Carolina. We spent almost every Friday and Saturday there. Sometimes we got to spend a whole week at a time. With a pair of special-order skis, I learned to water-ski at age four. By age eight or nine, I could slalom (on one ski).

My parents loved people. Because they were involved in many facets of church ministry, we frequently hosted people in our home or at the lake. My mom was the perfect hostess and an amazing cook. My parents always included my sister and me in their ministry.

Through the years, I was involved in oodles of church and school choirs, and my parents never missed an event. Even after I was married and teaching, they attended my middle school students' choral concerts.

I hope you can see through these few simple memories how big my parents' hearts were and how my sister and I never felt we didn't belong with them. My parents' pride and joy overflowed every time they told the story of how they "got" their two girls. The sparkle in their eyes let us know how they treasured us. Even after our mom developed dementia, our adoption stories stayed fresh in her mind and on her lips. She told our story over and over again with such excitement, as if she was telling it for the first time. It always brought a smile to her face and ours.

***

My favorite adoption story in the Old Testament is Moses's.

Read about his birth in Exodus 1:1–22 and 2:1–10.

Why did the Pharaoh of Egypt want to kill all the male Hebrew children?

_____

_____

_____

_____

How was Pharaoh's plan to be carried out?

_____

_____

_____

_____

Who delivered the Hebrew babies?

_____

_____

_____

_____

Why didn't the midwives want to do as Pharaoh commanded?

_____

_____

_____

_____

How did they avoid Pharaoh's evil plan?

_____

_____

_____

_____

Pharaoh later sent word to all the Hebrew women, telling them to do what?

_____

_____

_____

_____

What did Moses's mother initially do instead of casting him in the river to be drowned?

_____

_____

_____

_____

God always works in and weaves together the details of our lives. Digging into Moses's story, I found many parallels between our stories.

Though my birthmother wasn't a Hebrew woman, she was given an ultimatum after my birth. Instead of immediately giving in to the demand, she tried to keep me for three months, as Moses's mother did.

When circumstances proved too difficult, my birthmother put me up for adoption. Much later, I found out she had asked the adoption agency to place me in a Christian home. God answered her prayer fifty-seven days later. However, because it was a private adoption, she did not know if her prayers had been answered.

An Egyptian Pharaoh's daughter found baby Moses in his river basket, adopted him, and raised him in Pharaoh's palace. This was nothing short of God's divine design. God doesn't make mistakes. Every baby conceived is His creation, even if the conception is unplanned or is the result of some horrific, evil act. Every life conceived is a gift from God above, created with His unique purpose in mind.

Describe some of the details of your own story, proving God's presence and faithfulness in your life.

_____

_____

_____

_____

_____

_____

_____

_____

Read Exodus 2:1–10. Pay close attention to the miraculous details.

Is that not the sweetest gift ever? Even during a volatile situation, God not only kept this little one safe, but He also made a way for the baby's own mother to nurse him until he was weaned. When the time came, the child, not yet named, was taken to Pharaoh's daughter, and she adopted him and named him Moses. God had intricately involved Himself in the details of Moses's life, from knitting him together in his mother's womb (Psalm 139) to saving his life for the glorious purpose for which he was born.

Why did Pharaoh's daughter choose to name the child Moses?

_____

_____

_____

Moses was from the priestly tribe of Levi. These priests acted as liaisons between God and His people. Moses's life symbolized Jesus's life. Moses's purpose was to lead God's people out of slavery and into freedom, a foreshadowing of the Messiah, our perfect High Priest, setting us free from our bondage (slavery) to sin.

***

Details do matter, and we should pay attention to them. God has amazed me through the meanings of my name as He did with Moses. My birthmother named me Laura when I was born. After my adoption, my parents changed my name to Melanie Ann Cook. Searching the meanings of each name gave me another glimpse into God's sovereignty in my life.

- **Laura:** the feminine form of the Latin name Laurus, which means "laurel." It is a favorable name since ancient Romans used the leaves of laurel trees to create victors' garlands. (behindthename.com)

- **Melanie:** The French form of the Latin name Melania, derived from the Greek (*melaina*) meaning "black, dark." This was the name of a Roman saint who gave all her wealth to charity in the fifth century. A common name during the Middle Ages, the name eventually became rare. Interest in the name revived with the character Melanie Wilkes from the novel *Gone with the Wind* (1936) and the subsequent movie adaptation (1939). (behindthename.com)

- Seeing the movie when she was sixteen years old, my mother decided that, if she ever had a little girl, she would name her Melanie.

- **Ann:** The English form of Anne, used since the Middle Ages, though Ann became much more popular in the nineteenth century (behindthename.com). The biblical meaning for *Ann* is *favor* or *grace*. (sheknows.com)

God reveals Himself through the details of our lives, but we must seek Him to see Him. I began as Laura, named for laurel tree leaves used to make war-hero garlands. I learned much later in life that my birth mother battled hard to keep me before she chose to give me up—the loving option of adoption. I consider her a heroine. She deserves a victor's garland.

My parents legally changed my name on my birth certificate. My adoptive parents were allowed to choose a name for me, so my mother got her wish and named me Melanie after her favorite character in the movie, *Gone with the Wind.*

The name Melanie means black, or dark, and aren't we all born with a dark sin nature? I also received a middle name, Ann, which means favor or grace. My mom chose a name beginning with the letter A because she wanted her children to have their daddy's initials, MAC. Whether my mom knew the meaning of the name Ann or not, I'm not sure, but she chose a name of protection, a covering of grace. God can even use our names to proclaim His story of redemption and restoration. The word "coincidence" is not in God's vocabulary, so I believe even my name has significance in the story He's writing with my life.

***

Do some research of your name. Look up the original language, meaning, and any other details you can find. Research the biblical meaning. Does it fit your personality, story, or anything significant along your life's journey? Write your findings here.

_____

_____

_____

_____

_____

> The Lord your God is in your midst, a mighty one who will save; he will rejoice over you with gladness; he will quiet you by his love; he will exult over you with loud singing. (Zephaniah 3:17 ESV)

My favorite adoption story in the New Testament is ours—yours and mine.

Read Ephesians 1:1–14, Romans 8:1–17, and Galatians 4:1–7.

What common threads run through these passages?

_____

_____

_____

_____

What does the Holy Spirit have to do with our spiritual adoption?

_____

_____

_____

_____

Physical adoption is a precious gift wrapped in love—something the child doesn't usually ask for. Spiritual adoption is God's gift for all people, wrapped up in His love, grace, and mercy, through the sacrifice of His Son. It's a gift we can never earn and don't deserve. But we must ask for God's gift and then receive it with a surrendered heart.

If you've trusted Jesus Christ as your Savior and Lord, you are an adopted child of the King. He has brought you into His family and given you a new name. He whispers to your soul, "You are My beloved."

 And because you are sons, God has sent the Spirit of his Son into our hearts, crying, "Abba! Father!" So you are no longer a slave, but a son, and if a son, then an heir through God. (Galatians 4:6–7 ESV)

***

Having been born again by the blood of Jesus Christ, you are a forever child of God and an heir to His kingdom. Write a letter of thanksgiving to Him for adopting you into His forever family.

If you're unsure about your salvation, why not settle it today? Write a prayer of desire to become a child of the King. Confess your sins and choose to trust Christ as your Savior. Ask Him to be your Lord and the protector of your heart. If this is your prayer, share your good news with a friend this week. Below is an example to help you begin writing your prayer.

Dear Jesus, I confess that I am a sinner, and I know I cannot save myself from the consequences of my sin. I choose You as my Savior. I believe You came to die for me on the cross and have redeemed me through Your own precious blood and resurrection from the grave. Please forgive me for my sins. Although I don't deserve it, I accept Your gift of salvation by grace through faith. I want to follow You, Lord. I surrender my life to You today. Thank You for saving me and giving me new life. In Jesus's name I pray. Amen.

_____

_____

_____

_____

_____

_____

_____

_____

_____

_____

_____

_____

_____

_____

_____

_____

_____

_____

_____

_____

_____

_____

_____

_____

_____

_____

_____

_____

_____

_____

_____

_____

_____

#notguilty

#forgiven

#free

LESSON 5

Drenched in Grace

I was eighteen, holding hands in a large circle of believers, praying and singing praise songs. I didn't expect the uncontrollable tears flowing from my eyes. These tears were nothing like those that fell during the sweet moment when I received grace, sealing my eternal destiny. This was much deeper. Without warning, God opened wide the mercy gates of heaven and drenched me in grace.

***

During my freshman year at the University of South Carolina, I attended a different church than the one I'd grown up in. I was spiritually parched, and this body of believers ministered to my thirst. I lapped up every drop of truth I could hold, but my soul yearned for a fresh dousing of living water. As I stood among the crowd gathered in a circle of praise and prayer, I silently pleaded with God, asking Him to show Himself to me. The longer I stood there, the stronger the longing in my soul grew. I sensed the Lord pulling me into Himself with an urgency, though I was unaware of all He was up to. Even though a large gathering of new friends filled the room, I felt as if I stood alone in the presence of Jesus.

Then, without warning, my secret began to play over and over in my mind. The guilt roared to life again, and I wrestled with fear and shame. *Why does my secret still haunt me?*

The heaviness of my secret pressed in harder than ever.

But so did my Savior.

While the enemy condemned me, Jesus comforted me. The enemy did not want my thirst quenched, so he did everything in his power to distract me from this sacred moment. However, the more Satan tried to distract, the more Jesus leaned right into me—into my hurt, into my shame, into my secret—with His arms wrapped around me. My Savior gave me a glimpse of how extravagantly He loves me and how He had always been with me. Jesus never abandoned me. This truth overwhelmed me.

He saw me.

As tears trickled down my face, Jesus didn't accuse me or appear disappointed. Instead, His grace flowed like a waterfall, splashing mercy all over me. The feeling exhilarated me so much, it took my breath. It felt like a private baptism. The most amazing thing about this moment? No one else knew it was happening. I believe God gave me a powerful visual of what His Holy Spirit had already done in my heart.

Grace changed me.

Grace healed me.

Grace resuscitated me, breathing life back into my soul and filling me with joy—the real flooding-my-soul kind of joy.

I'll never forget the night when buckets of grace washed over me privately, smack-dab in the middle of a crowd. Since then, I've never been the same.

***

We find powerful grace encounters throughout the pages of Scripture. Let's examine two of those encounters. The first one, like mine, happens in a crowd.

Read Luke 8:40–48.

What had this woman been dealing with for twelve years?

_____

_____

Who had she been to for healing?

_____

_____

What happened to cause Jesus to turn His attention toward this woman?

_____

_____

How do you think she felt when Jesus noticed her?

_____

_____

What was essential for her healing?

_____

_____

Jesus saw her, even though the great crowd pushed around Him. He felt healing power leave His body. Jesus looked into her heart, saw her faith, and then healed her completely. He forgave her sins. He filled her with joy—something no other healer could do.

 And he said to her, "Daughter, your faith has made you well; go in peace." (Luke 8:48 ESV)

***

Now let's look into a more private grace encounter.

Read John 4:1–29.

Why had this woman gone to the well?

_____

Why was the well the perfect setting for this conversation?

_____

Who did the woman suspect might be lesser than the Messiah? (v. 12)?

_____

Why is this question significant, especially in the context of our studies of Jacob?

_____

_____

What had she used for years to try to fill her emptiness?

_____

What was amazing to her about Jesus?

_____

Pleasure can deceive. We run after what we think will satisfy us in the moment, but after we taste it, the faux satisfaction only fuels our desire for more empty pleasures. In Genesis chapter 3, the devil ravaged Adam and Eve with deceit. The only remedy is an encounter with the lover of our souls—the only One who satisfies our longing for real pleasure. His name is Jesus.

Jesus knew everything about her, including her failed marriages, and yet . . .

He sought her out.

He drew her to Himself.

He forgave her sins.

Because she believed, she was never the same.

> Jesus said to her, "Everyone who drinks of this water will be thirsty again, but whoever drinks of the water that I will give him will never be thirsty again. The water that I will give him will become in him a spring of water welling up to eternal life." (John 4:13–14 ESV)

Read verses 27–30.

After the conversation between Jesus and the woman at the well, what did she do?

_____

_____

Skip down and read verses 39–42.

What was the result of this woman telling her story?

_____

_____

_____

***

Do you need a grace dousing? Why not ask God for a glimpse of yourself at the foot of the cross through His eyes today?

What's your grace story?

_____

_____

_____

_____

What could happen when you tell others your story?

_____

_____

_____

_____

In the space provided, write a prayer of thanksgiving for the grace you've received and for the glimpses He's given you along your journey.

_____

_____

_____

_____

_____

_____

_____

_____

_____

_____

_____

_____

_____

_____

I have found the one whom my soul loves.
Song of Solomon 3:4

LESSON 6

The Man of My Prayers, Not My Dreams

Late one cold January night during my senior year of high school, I got up on my knees in my bed. With tears streaming down my face, I poured out a prayer like never before. "God, I don't want to play this dating game anymore. I'm tired of the wooing, the winning, the walking in and out of relationships. It's old and wearisome. I know I'm only seventeen, but my way of finding my forever someone is not going well. So God, if You have anyone in mind, I surrender complete control of my future to You." Then I laid my head on my pillow, curled up under the covers, and slept like a baby.

***

Two weeks after I laid it all before Jesus at my bed altar, God answered this seventeen-year-old's cry. However, not with the man of my dreams, but with the man of my prayers.

God answered my desperate prayer in an Ephesians 3:20 kind of way.

Write Ephesians 3:20 in the space provided.

_____

_____

_____

This verse expresses exactly how God brought my husband to me—giving me more than I ever dreamed, hoped for, or imagined. This is who our Creator is: the true God who exceeds our wildest dreams, lavishing His love on us in unexpected and surprising ways.

> And whatever you ask in prayer, you will receive, if you have faith. (Matthew 21:22 ESV)

***

Let's look at another weary woman's heart and listen to her prayer. Her name is Hannah, and she's pleading with God to give her something she desperately desires.

Read (and listen to) 1 Samuel 1.

Describe Hannah's situation.

_____

_____

_____

_____

Who made her situation more difficult to bear?

_____

Where did Hannah choose to pour out her heart to the Lord?

_____

How did she cry out to God—loudly or silently?

_____

What was Hannah's specific request of the Lord?

_____

_____

_____

What did Hannah vow to give to God if He chose to answer her prayer?

_____

How did God answer Hannah's prayer?

_____

Describe a time when you've prayed a heart-wrenching prayer. What was your request? Did you add a promise to your prayer as Hannah did? If so, did you keep it?

_____

_____

_____

_____

_____

_____

_____

How did Hannah approach the Lord differently than we sometimes do?
Share your thoughts.

_____

_____

_____

_____

_____

> Then the woman [Hannah] went on her way and ate, and her
> face was no longer sad. (1 Samuel 1:18 ESV)

Before Hannah came before the Lord, she had already made a decision.
If He opened her womb and gave her a child, she would release the child
back to Him to serve in the presence of Eli, the priest.

What a display of faith.

What a heart of courage.

What a sacrifice of love.

I don't remember making a vow like Hannah's when I asked the Lord to bring me the man He wanted me to marry. But I knew that, if God answered my cry, I could trust His choice. I would be forever grateful for "the one" He had chosen for me.

When do we first read of Hannah telling her husband about her vow? What did she say?

_____

_____

_____

_____

_____

Were you surprised by Elkanah's response? Why or why not?

_____

_____

Elkanah's seemingly calm response surprises me. He clearly had a strong faith in God. He must have known they were doing the right thing by keeping Hannah's promise to the Lord. The Scriptures don't give any other insight into their private conversations during the next months, but I imagine their decision was difficult.

Could I have left my firstborn, the one I had spent years praying for? The precious one I had already bonded with, fallen in love with, and adored while I inhaled his sweet baby scent? The one whose little fingers wrapped around mine as I fed him and rocked him to sleep? Could I give back the one who kicked his little feet as I sang to him? The one who had made me a mother?

I'm not sure I could have.

But Hannah and Elkanah did.

What do you cry out to God for today? Write out your prayer. Then pray, even if you must push past anguish and resentment. Come to Him with an open heart of surrender, a sure faith, strong courage, and deep love. No matter how He chooses to answer, He has only your good and His glory in mind.

***

God answered my cry within two weeks.

During my senior year in high school, I joined a singing group that traveled to churches around the state. My best friend, Steph, was in the group with me. One day she said, "If you'll give me vocal lessons, I'll introduce you to Rick Shull, that cute guy in my church."

I didn't know Rick, although he lived around the corner from me. We had not attended the same high school because he'd moved during his senior year and finished at his old school. He had graduated from my rival school two years earlier. I'd seen Rick from a distance as I rode my bike by his house, trying to catch a glimpse of the cute guy in the neighborhood. He was usually playing basketball in his driveway and looked good from a distance.

I agreed to Steph's offer. She arranged a double date.

Finally, the big day arrived. When Rick came to the front door, his icy-blue eyes were the first thing I noticed. He sported Calvin Klein jeans, a tweed blazer over a sweater and a button-down oxford, and Bass penny loafers, and he smelled of Chaps cologne.

In the driveway, he opened the door of his tan Buick Regal for me, and the four of us soon headed to our first stop—a Bible study for youth and college kids. Our second stop was a quaint little Pizza Inn.

The evening couldn't have gone better. Too soon, it was time to go home. Rick dropped off Steph and her date and then headed back to my house. There we sat in the car and talked for a few moments. Then things turned a little awkward.

"Do you want me to walk you to the door?"

No guy had asked me that before. I said, "No, thanks. I think I can handle it."

And guess what? He let me open my own car door and walk alone to my house, flabbergasted and confused. He hadn't even tried to kiss me goodnight, not even on the cheek.

This was not how dates were supposed to end.

After my sarcastic response, I wasn't sure he would call me for another date. I wasn't sure I wanted him to. It was definitely not love at first sight. He was not the man of my dreams.

But wait. Remember what I said about Rick being the man of my prayers?

I don't think any girl had ever responded as I had. In my defense, he'd caught me off guard. I'd spoken the first thought that entered my mind.

However, it must have not bothered him too much, because the gorgeous guy with the icy-blue eyes and the great-smelling cologne did ask me out again.

Later, Rick explained our date's strange ending. "When a guy asks a girl if she wants him to walk her to the door, and she says 'Yes,' then she wants a goodnight kiss. If she says 'No,' she doesn't want a kiss."

I must have missed that piece of dating info.

God continued to affirm that Rick was the man of my prayers. For the next five years, God began to grow us up in our love for Him and each other. No one could believe we dated that long. Our college pastor called him one day after we had dated for several years. In his deep, former-DJ voice, the pastor said, "Rick, this is the Lord speaking. Marry that girl!" We had dated so long that, if Rick had bent down to tie his shoe in my presence, I would have shouted, "Yes, I'll marry you!"

Rick did propose in July of 1984, and we were married on February 23, 1985, in the presence of over 500 witnesses.

***

Rick's trustworthiness is one of the ways I know Rick is the man of my prayers. Wild animals couldn't pull a secret from him. I know. I've tried, in wild-animal fashion. How many of us can keep secrets? Probably only a handful.

Even though my husband has always been trustworthy, I never felt the need to divulge my deepest, darkest secret. But soon after the forgiveness encounter with my perpetrator, Rick made an innocent comment. While we watched a movie about sexual abuse, Rick said he couldn't understand how anyone could keep something like that to herself for so many years.

My heart sank. The enemy went to work, planting seeds of shame and guilt in my heart, where the Spirit had recently uprooted my hate, anger, and bitterness through the power of forgiveness. Immediately, Satan convinced me I could never tell my husband because he simply wouldn't understand. Then Satan's favorite weapon of fear crept in and whispered, "If you tell your husband, he will never see you in the same way again."

So I didn't. I hid my secret for at least eight more years.

***

Let's continue with Hannah's story. Read 1 Samuel 2.

After Hannah followed through with her vow, what did she do?

_____

Do any of the words or phrases in Hannah's prayer stand out to you?
Write them down and explain why you chose each one.

_____

_____

_____

_____

_____

***

I started teaching private piano lessons while I was in college and took
it up again when I left the classroom to be a full-time mom. I loved the
freedom of arranging my schedule so I could spend quality time with
our son. When he was four, we moved into our third house, my in-laws'
home, because they had decided to downsize. This is the house where
Rick lived when we met. It was also the house in which he proposed.
Shortly after moving, I became pregnant with our second child, a girl.
We could not have been more thrilled.

Then my husband acquired his real estate appraisal license. This created
a new branch in the family business. This position didn't offer health
insurance, so I had to return to the classroom. I was not happy about
leaving my son in childcare. I allowed bitterness to creep in, and my
attitude began to change toward this wonderful, godly man of my
prayers. The door of my heart slammed shut—again.

How did this happen to me repeatedly? Could I not learn this lesson and move on?

As my resentment toward my husband grew stronger, Rick knew he needed to address my attitude. In a stern but compassionate voice, he said, "You're not angry about going back to work as much as you are resentful and bitter toward me for a situation I have no control over."

Oh, don't you just hate it when they're right? I know women who endlessly pray for their husbands to become the spiritual leaders of their homes. However, even when both spouses are seeking Christ, no marriage is immune from struggles.

I realized I needed someone to blame for my bitterness and self-made misery. My husband was the unfortunate recipient.

Anger unmanaged will result in a bitter spirit.

Not long after Rick forced me to stare into the mirror of my heart, a friend invited me to attend Kay Arthur's study, "Lord, Only You Can Change Me." Little did I know that those next six weeks would again spark divinely appointed counseling sessions with my Savior. During that time, he continued to teach me that forgiveness is key, especially in marriage.

This time I needed the forgiveness key because of my attitude toward my husband—for wounding him with my words and for refusing to follow his leadership for our family. I asked him to forgive me, and he graciously did. This unlocked the door to my heart and allowed joy to flow again. Rick promised that my job would be temporary—no more than five years. After that, he would be able to provide insurance for our family again, and I would be back home with the kiddos.

Those next five years of teaching were some of the hardest and some of the best. I built lifelong friendships with students, faculty, and administrators. God used me to build a successful music program, and

He gave me many opportunities to grow up in my faith, to seek godly wisdom, and to learn to trust Him.

During the third year, the doctor put me on eight weeks of bedrest while I was pregnant with our daughter. After her birth, I cried every day when I dropped her off at the babysitter's and left for work. Leaving my kids was the hardest thing I've ever had to do.

Two years later, on the morning of the first day of year five, I gently reminded my husband of his promise. Eyes wide with mock surprise, he said, "Has it been five years already?"

> Put on then, as God's chosen ones, holy and beloved, compassionate hearts, kindness, humility, meekness, and patience, bearing with one another and, if one has a complaint against another, forgiving each other; as the Lord has forgiven you, you also must forgive. (Colossians 3:12–13 ESV)

When I left the teaching profession this time, our daughter was two and our son was seven. I began working at our church as associate minister of music and learned my perpetrator had moved back into our area. Even though I had forgiven him six years earlier, I hadn't forgotten his moment of misconduct in my life. God is the only one with the capacity to forgive and forget (Psalm 103:10–12).

I still had not uttered a word to my husband about my secret, the nightmares, or my appointment with my perpetrator. But now, with my offender living nearby, I couldn't keep my secret any longer. I had to tell my husband. Together, we needed to set safe boundaries.

So, one night, when I could not bear the burden of my secret any longer, I got on my knees beside my husband's chair in our den. Between sobs, I told him what had happened to me many years earlier. I revealed my motives for keeping the secret, admitted to my nightmares, my fear, my anger. I described the phone call and my visit with my offender. I told him the whole story until it dangled out there between us in the silence.

Then, with tenderness and tears in those beautiful blue eyes, my husband hugged me and held me. I have never known anyone with such a compassionate heart. He never made light of my hurt or questioned me about details. He simply loved me.

I believe God chose Rick for me because He knew who I needed to walk with me and love me through my story. God knew I needed a man who would be His answer to my prayers rather than a prince from my fairytale dreams. He knew I needed someone who would love me unconditionally, work through the heartache with me, hold me when the tears flowed, and never look at me differently because of my past. My husband is one of my most treasured gifts, and I give thanks to God for bringing him into my life via my prayer of surrender.

***

Now that we've examined Hannah's heart-wrenching prayer, and I invited you into mine, do you have an ache to give to the Lord? As you've seen, bitterness can sneak into our hearts when we least expect it, especially when accompanied with disappointment and unmet expectations. To keep our hearts from slamming shut with bitterness, we must surrender our plans to God, as Hannah did. We can trust Him, because He knows what's best, and He knows every detail of our stories.

Write out 1 Thessalonians 5:18.

_____

In the journaling space provided, write a prayer of thanksgiving. Even if you're going through hard times, praise God anyway. List some of the gifts He's given you. Thank Him from a sincere and grateful heart. You may not see the whole picture now, but you can rest, knowing God always works things out for good for those who love Him and are called according to His purpose (Romans 8:28).

Search me, O God, and know my heart;
Try me and know my anxieties;
And see if there is any wicked way in me,
And lead me in the way everlasting.

Psalm 139:23-24 NKJV

LESSON 7

Forgiving Is Holy Art

Many years have passed since my forgiveness encounter. Although I've regained my freedom and joy, I still have opportunities to offer and receive the key of forgiveness.

Forgiving is holy art.

To be holy is to be "set apart" for God's purpose: to imitate His Son. Becoming a holy masterpiece begins with our initial salvation experience and continues with the process of sanctification.

The Holy Spirit is the Master Artist. Every heart surrendered to Jesus Christ becomes a diamond in the rough. The Holy Spirit refines, shapes, and chisels until the brilliant light of the Savior reflects from every angle. We make glorious progress with each obedient act of faith. The Holy Spirit's artwork of sanctification will continue until we see Jesus face to face.

Until then, we are diamonds in the making.

 From the beginning God has chosen you for salvation through sanctification by the Spirit and through belief in the truth. (2 Thessalonians 2:13)

The art of forgiving is part of the sanctification process.

Read Luke 23:1–49.

Jesus gasped for breath on the cross and then bellowed out, "Father, forgive them; for they do not know what they are doing" (Luke 23:34 NASB).

Christ's emptying of Himself to redeem the world was holy art perfected. By spilling the red of His blood, He white-washed the canvases of our darkened hearts. With His mercy, He forgave us all. With His final breath, He set us free. No suffering on earth will ever compare to the glorious sufferings of Christ. He calls His children to share in His sufferings as a part of our transformation, becoming like Him in His glory. Holy hearts perfected.

 And if children, then heirs—heirs of God and fellow heirs with Christ, provided we suffer with him in order that we may also be glorified with him. (Romans 8:17 ESV)

Forgiving and receiving forgiveness is the holy art we must practice often. Through forgiveness, we polish the Son's image imprinted on our hearts. We imitate Christ when we forgive.

Through the years, I've had to practice this holy art more times than I like to admit. He's still working on me.

Each time we empty ourselves, the process gets easier. Not easy, but easier. It's always hard to admit we're wrong, no matter who we say it to. Saying "I'm sorry" is only the beginning. Growth comes when we learn to recognize the need to ask for or extend the forgiveness key and then do it as soon as possible.

Once a coworker accused me of being the most ungodly woman he had ever known. The accusation ripped through my heart. I couldn't speak. My stomach knotted as if I'd taken a blow to the gut, and I was afraid I would throw up. Later, as I processed this event, I thought, *What happened? Why does he think that? Sure, I'm not perfect, but if this person sees me as ungodly, do others see me that way too?*

Now, I am not one who hides my thoughts and emotions. You know how some people need a filter for their mouths? Well, I need one for my face. It's easy to read my mind by looking at my expression.

I can only imagine the look I gave him. I'd seen his unwarranted, sometimes out-of-control anger many times in public. But now, hurled directly at me in a private encounter, it hit hard and fast.

Even though he was lying, Satan hurled rapid-fire doubt darts at me. It happened so fast, I needed to take immediate action. Had I given that impression to any of my other co-workers? However, before I made a move, I approached the throne of grace. A spiritual war raged, and I knew I had to fight this battle on my knees.

I cried out for God to search my heart, my thoughts, and my actions. I confessed anything and everything I could think of that might resemble the ungodliness the man had accused me of. I knew I had acted in a disrespectful manner through my facial expressions, so I asked my Savior for forgiveness for my attitude. Then I asked for guidance in handling the awkward and painful situation.

> For we do not wrestle against flesh and blood, but against the rulers, against the authorities, against the cosmic powers over this present darkness, against the spiritual forces of evil in the heavenly places. Therefore take up the whole armor of God, that you may be able to withstand in the evil day, and having done all, to stand firm. (Ephesians 6:12–13 ESV)

Convicted of my disrespectful attitude toward my accuser, I began to draft an email. I sent it to everyone my accuser said I'd transgressed against, as well as to the accuser himself. With sincere apologies, I asked for each person's forgiveness. I knew I couldn't move on until my relationship with each person had been restored, if need be. I was confident my conscience was clear of any wrongdoing.

My accuser did not respond to my plea for forgiveness. However, everyone else seemed confused as to why I asked for their forgiveness. Their response affirmed that I had done the right thing. Clearly the man had falsely accused me of behaving in an ungodly fashion toward them.

This holy art of forgiveness was difficult and gut-wrenching. But because I had cleared my conscience of any wrongdoing, I knew I had acted in obedience.

***

The holy art of asking for and extending forgiveness is an outward reflection of an inward transformation. Being aware of the moment we've hurt someone, and immediately recognizing the need to restore the relationship, is a sign that our faith in Christ is growing.

 For to set the mind on the flesh is death, but to set the mind on the Spirit is life and peace. (Romans 8:6 ESV)

Christ, who sits on the mercy seat, understands forgiveness better than anyone. While on earth, Jesus walked the streets of towns and villages, teaching, healing, and restoring hearts. He forgave people for their sins, changing their lives forever.

A beautiful example of transformation is the account of the paralytic and his friends who lowered him through the roof into the place where Jesus was teaching.

Read Luke 5:17–26.

Who was among those listening to Jesus's teachings in this passage?

_____

_____

What was Jesus filled with according to verse 17?

_____

When the friends of the paralytic lowered him into the center of the crowd before Jesus, what did Jesus notice before He healed the man?

_____

When we come into the presence of Jesus, He wants to see our faith. Practicing the holy art of forgiveness toward those who accuse, abuse, and hurt us takes great faith. We must believe God will be faithful to make something beautiful out of the mess sin has caused. Our obedience in practicing this holy art form brings glory to the Father, casting streams of light even into the darkest of hearts.

Read Luke 11:33–35.

Where does a lamp belong, and where does it not belong?

_____

_____

Why is this important?

_____

_____

Why do you think the eye is called the lamp of the body?

_____

_____

In verse 35, we are given a warning. What is this warning, and what do you think it means for us today?

_____

_____

In verse 36, what happens if we obey this passage?

_____

Using a Bible concordance or other Bible resource, list several Scriptures that refer to Christ as the Light. Beside each one, describe how you think these verses connect with Luke 11:36.

_____

_____

_____

_____

What is the outcome of our obedience in being bright, and why does this matter to Christ?

_____

_____

We will never fully understand what it means to forgive until we bend our knees at the foot of the cross and embrace Jesus's words: "Father, forgive them, because they do not know what they are doing" (Luke 23:34).

I love that this verse is in the present tense. Jesus spoke not only of the soldiers and the people who literally crucified Him, but also of every person who had come before and everyone who would come after. The sins of the whole world nailed Him to the cross. The sacrificial Lamb, broken and spilled out for you, for me, bridged the great chasm sin had carved between the Father and us. Now all who believe by faith can stand before the Father, covered in the righteousness of Christ, justified and forgiven.

I am forgiven.

You are forgiven.

Christ breathed His last after speaking three powerful words, "It is finished" (John 19:30). The sin debt we owed was now and forever paid in full. Hallelujah!

***

No one on earth has ever suffered or will ever suffer as Christ did. We are called to share in His sufferings, but nothing we go through will ever compare to the excruciating pain Christ endured for us. In lesson 1, we read Isaiah 53. Today, let's remember the wounds Christ took for us.

Read Isaiah 53.

The wounding of Christ became healing for us.

 And he said to all, "If anyone would come after me, let him deny himself and take up his cross daily and follow me." (Luke 9:23 ESV)

Christ calls us to pick up our crosses daily and follow Him.

What do our crosses look like?

_____

_____

We're called to carry our crosses for the "killing of self" every day. What do you think this means?

_____

_____

Read Romans 12:1–2.

What is a living sacrifice, according to these verses?

_____

_____

_____

When we nail our selfish desires to our daily crosses, Satan cannot deter us from becoming who Christ wants us to be. Death to self can come only through consistent prayer and the washing of the mind with the Word. When we lay down "self" and kill it, then God's resurrection power can flow freely through us. His blood breaks the power of our canceled sin. Unlocked hearts can now unleash joy every moment of every day. This is what living free in Christ is all about.

We could literally change the world if we'd begin each morning with a prayer like this:

Good morning, Lord! Thank You for another breath, another day to live with and for You. I want to begin this day by nailing "self" to my daily cross. I confess my selfish desires before You and ask You to be my only desire today. I want to be a pleasing aroma to You. Make my burden light so I can follow You wholeheartedly in all I do and say. This is my sacred act of spiritual worship. Let my life be a living sacrifice, holy and acceptable to You this day. In the name of Jesus, I pray. Amen.

***

God continued taking me into deeper waters to learn to trust Him more. As my faith grew stronger, God asked me again to extend the key of forgiveness. In the final chapter of this study, I invite you to come with me on one last adventure of trust and obedience. This journey landed me on the doorstep of a stranger—one I never would have dreamed of approaching—to unlock another heart and unleash more of God's joy.

_____

_____

_____

_____

_____

_____

_____

_____

_____

_____

_____

_____

_____

_____

_____

_____

_____

_____

Weeping may endure for a night, but joy comes in the morning.

Psalm 30:5b

LESSON 8

Full-Circle: Joy Unleashed

"If you ever want to find your birthmother, it's okay with us."

What? Why after forty years would my parents suddenly give their blessing for something I had never asked for? Not once had I ever dreamed of searching for her.

***

Standing in the parking lot of a local restaurant after celebrating my fortieth adopted-day, my aging parents caught me off guard with this never-sought-after blessing. I'd shared my adoption story in numerous concert settings and often said how I would love to fill in some of the gaps of my story. Perhaps that prompted my parents to offer me this blessing. I only made those comments for the benefit of my audiences, not because I seriously intended to search for the woman who'd brought me into this world. The family God had chosen for me was perfect. I didn't need to seek out anyone else.

I'm not sure I want more information, Lord. I doubt my papers will reveal more than we already know. Are You saying I should request them? Oh, I don't know what to do. Lord, help me. Is this You working or not?

Since a private lawyer had handled my adoption, we knew little about my birth parents. We knew only where I was born and that I had come from a musical family. I was not sure what, if anything else, we could uncover. However, the Spirit prompted me to move ahead and take this step of obedience. I was learning how to identify when the Spirit spoke to me, and the gnawing in my gut has become my sure signal. Still, it took me several months to send in the request form, along with thirty-five dollars, and ask for my Department of Social Services (DSS) papers.

Sending a request form didn't mean I was signing up to meet my biological mother. It meant only that I hoped to fill in some of the puzzle pieces so I could share more of the story during ministry opportunities. I can imagine the Lord smiling as if He was eating a banana sideways, because He knew what was waiting for me around the corner.

Within a few weeks, I received a letter from DSS. I ripped open the envelope. The letter stated I would not receive any information for fifty-two weeks because they were so backlogged with requests.

Are you kidding me? A whole year? What's up with this, Lord?

 But they who wait for the Lord shall renew their strength; they shall mount up with wings like eagles; they shall run and not be weary; they shall walk and not faint. (Isaiah 40:31 ESV)

God is never early, nor is He late. His timing is always perfect. He sees the whole picture from His heavenly throne. We, on the other hand, can see only one step at a time, so we must trust Him. In these uncertain moments He stretches our faith. And boy, was He stretching mine.

I had spent the last forty years learning to trust God. I had taken many risks of faith. He continually worked in me to grow my faith and to strengthen me spiritually. Although I didn't know what lay ahead, I continued walking, waiting, and holding on to His dear hand. I put the letter to the side and forgot about it.

***

One of those tough trust lessons was presented to the disciples soon after the crucifixion.

Read John 20.

The greatest event in all of history had just occurred. What was it?

_____

The disciples had been on the adventure of a lifetime with the Messiah for three years, but they weren't sure what to do now. So they returned to the place where they felt safe and secure. They had answered His call to follow Him. They had obeyed and left everything in order to experience life with the Savior. I can't imagine their wounded hearts as they watched their teacher, rabbi, and best friend hanging from a cross.

When the disciples gathered in verse 19, why did they lock the doors?

_____

_____

Even Jesus's disciples—those who knew Him in a deep and powerful way—were afraid. They'd watched Him perform miracle after miracle. They'd seen the impossible happen. But they still gave in to fear and doubt. How much easier is it for us to be filled with fear and doubt since we have not seen Him with our physical eyes?

Jesus knew the disciples' anxious hearts, so He walked through literal walls and into their fear. He calmed their restlessness with His presence, proving His resurrected life. He gave them hope for a future, something to live for, and a powerful message to proclaim.

And He does the same for us.

In chapter 21, John tells us Jesus again revealed Himself to the disciples at the Sea of Tiberias. Even though they had seen the resurrected Jesus, Peter and some of the others decided to go back to what they knew—catching fish. They returned to the place where they felt comfortable, unaware that the risen Lord would show up in their ordinary lives to stretch their faith for what was to come.

Read John 21.

What did Jesus ask the disciples to do after they answered His question with, "No, we haven't caught a thing"?

_____

Jesus didn't ask them to change their nets, swap out their bait, or tweak their skills. He didn't ask them to pack up and go to another lake. Wasn't it the same water? Weren't they using the same nets?

What do you think was Jesus's purpose in asking them to drop their nets on the opposite side of the boat?

_____

_____

***

While I struggled to decide whether to leave the Christian female vocal group called Together for Him, God led me to John chapter twenty-one. There Jesus instructed his disciples to cast their nets on the other side of the boat. He used those same words to confirm my decision to walk away from a ministry I'd loved for years. Jesus didn't tell me to stop singing. He called me to drop my nets into another spot in His sea of opportunity.

With a trusting heart and a step of faith, I believed God's Word and obeyed. If I had not "cast my nets on the other side of the boat," *Living Real Magazine* would not exist today. Publishing this magazine has been my greatest faith adventure. God has affirmed my lesson so many times that I've not only learned to identify His voice, but I've learned to act on it as well. If I hadn't obeyed with the magazine, you wouldn't be studying this book. Every step of obedience leads us to the next step, and the next, and the next.

What does the Holy Spirit's voice sound like to you? How do you know it's His voice tugging at your heart to move forward in obedience? Describe a time when you knew the Spirit had called you to do something.

_____

_____

_____

_____

_____

As I began to discern the Spirit's voice from the enemy's, I learned that God never tells us anything that does not agree with His Word. He can speak to us through other people, and in other ways as well, but we must know His truth so we can determine whose voice we've heard.

***

While I waited for my DSS papers to arrive, God worked in ways unknown to me. During the next fifty-two weeks, He steered me and my faith into deeper waters where I couldn't touch the bottom. He led me into a place of total reliance on Him. God knew my daddy, my earthly hero, would need my help as his health would continue to deteriorate. He knew my sister and I would have to make the hard choice of moving both our parents into an assisted living facility. And He knew my sweet daddy would pass away within months of the move and that my mom would need extra care as she adjusted to life without him.

I didn't know how exhausting caregiving could be, but the Author of my story knew. Nothing happens in our lives that the Master doesn't allow. In short, God protected my heart because I would need spiritual and emotional strength for the year ahead.

Ten months after my dad passed, I stopped at the mailbox on a Friday morning and pulled out a large manila envelope with a DSS return address.

My adoption files.

I realized I had requested the information exactly fifty-two weeks ago.

With a trembling hand, I set the letter on the seat next to me. I hadn't expected to feel this scared, excited, and nervous about a document that might fill in the blanks of a past I'd never wanted to pursue.

Until now.

I headed to work at the church, deciding to open the letter at my desk. There, I said a quick prayer, opened the envelope, and slid out the papers.

First, I noticed several solid black Sharpie lines through much of the information. It didn't surprise me, since I knew a closed adoption file cannot reveal names, birthdates, places, or any other personal information.

As I began to read, I was stunned, because somehow I was even able to read the words marked out in black.

I could see every word on every page through every Sharpie mark.

Every sibling's name, every birthdate, and even details of my birthmother's location when she decided to give me up—they all stared back at me through the permanent ink marks.

I set down the pages and closed my eyes. Lord, why would You unveil so many details that I'm not supposed to see?

God was obviously up to something significant, something way beyond my comprehension. I'd never had an inkling that any of this information would surface, but He chose to reveal it anyway. I continued my conversation with God, asking Him to let me know why He had shown all this to me.

During this time, our church was in a transition period, as we were seeking a pastor. Two days after my discovery, the visiting pastor preached about Psalm 139 in his sermon. As I've said before, I always use verses 13–16 to frame my adoption story. I call them my "Scripture picture."

> For you formed my inward parts; you knitted me together in my mother's womb. Your eyes saw my unformed substance; in your book were written, every one of them, the days that were formed for me, when as yet there was none of them. (Psalm 139:13, 16 ESV)

Was this a coincidence?

Then the pastor included verses 11–12, which I had never paid much attention to. These verses impacted me because I know God doesn't work in a happenstance fashion.

> If I say, "Surely the darkness shall cover me, and the light about me be night," even the darkness is not dark to you; the night is bright as the day, for darkness is as light with you. (Psalm 139: 11–12 ESV)

This revelation made me again wonder why God had revealed so much information. From the dates revealed in my papers, I estimated my birthmother's age to be mid- to late sixties.

Was she in bad health? Did she wonder what had happened to me? Maybe this whole adventure had nothing to do with me. Maybe it had everything to do with her and her needs.

Whatever the answers, I knew the Spirit had opened this door for a reason. However, I wasn't sure how to walk through it.

In our small group after worship, I shared a bit of what had taken place, asking everyone to pray that I would hear the Spirit's voice clearly and would know what to do. All afternoon I prayed. I reviewed the dates and names. Then I noticed, on the bottom of the first page, my birthmother's request: *Please place her in a Christian home.*

God had honored her request. When I was five, I asked Jesus to be my Savior. He has been my best and closest friend ever since. I believe my salvation journey began early for many reasons, but I never thought He might use my story in the most miraculous of ways.

I decided to try and contact a brother named Jimmy. Even if he was married, his name would have remained the same. I found a phone number, but before I dialed, I told God, "These people need to know Jesus or at least know about Him, because if not, they'll think I'm crazy."

A gentleman answered the phone, and I asked to speak to Jimmy. I did not disclose who I was or why I was calling. Without asking me any questions, the man on the other end gave me the phone number of Jimmy's older sister, Macy. He said she would be able to put me in contact with him. I thought his comment odd, but I was making progress and was grateful. Later, I found out the man on the other end of the phone was a family member and had been instrumental in my birthmother choosing the loving option of adoption.

The next phone call was nothing short of another miracle. Remember when I told God I needed them to know about Jesus? When I called, a man answered the phone and said, "Macy's not home. She's at Vacation Bible School and should be home in a couple of hours."

Thank You, Jesus!

I asked him to have her return my call, but I didn't dare say why.

Thinking I had quite a while before Macy would return my call, I left to pick up my daughter from youth group. While I waited in the parking lot, my phone rang. Macy's number popped up on the screen.

After I'd confirmed I had the right person, I took a deep breath and disclosed the reason for my call. "I'm Baby Laura, the child your mom gave up for adoption many years ago."

Macy screamed into the phone as if she'd just won a Publishers Clearing House sweepstakes. When I brought the phone back to my ringing ear, she said, "I can't believe it's you. Our mom has talked about you all our lives. She even wanted us to search for you the moment we got a computer."

I still get chills thinking about Macy's overwhelming response and my answered prayers. Macy and I talked for about a half an hour and discovered we had much in common: children, music, and of course, Jesus. During our conversation, God threw me another treat to chew on. Macy worked as a secretary in a Baptist church where she also sang in the choir.

The next day included lots of emails back and forth, leading up to another phone call from Macy, confirming the time I would call her mom—my birthmother. All four of the siblings (one older brother, one older sister, and two younger sisters) wanted to be in the room with their mother when she got the call. We decided I would call at six o'clock that evening.

Before we hung up, Macy paused. "You need to know something about Mom before you call. She has been bedridden for ten years and has suffered from depression for forty-three."

By this time, I was forty-three years old. Coincidence? No. God's vocabulary doesn't include the word.

The most amazing detail is God's affirmation that I was doing what He wanted me to do. Earlier in the day, Macy shared that during our phone conversation on Sunday, her sister was visiting with their mom, who said, "I hope Laura can forgive me one day."

As six o'clock approached, I prayed for courage and strength. I didn't want to cry. I wanted to stay strong for this heartbroken woman who thought she had done me wrong. I wasn't angry with her or bitter toward her. Rather, I was deeply grateful for the way God had orchestrated my life. I simply wanted to thank her for making the hard choice. I wanted to help her find some peace.

I picked up the phone and dialed the number, never having thought I would make this call. After several rings, the woman who'd carried me for nine months and then tried to care for me for about three, answered the phone.

Her frail-sounding voice is what I remember. I can only imagine the view from the other end of the phone. Four adult siblings sitting around their mother's bed, anxiously awaiting her initial response as she heard, for the first time in over forty years, the voice of the baby girl she had given up so long ago.

"Hi, Mrs. Nancy. This is Melanie. I'm Baby Laura."

For the next little while she riddled me with questions about my life, my parents, and my family. She tried hard to bridge the forty-three-year span separating us. It's difficult to put into words what the unveiling was like, but I knew I was being obedient to the Lord, and that caused joy to well up inside me.

Before we hung up, she said, "I need to know two things. Are you happy?"

"Yes, ma'am."

Then she asked the more important question. "Are you a Christian?"

"Yes, ma'am. I am."

I continued to assure her of my happiness and my thankfulness for the home God had placed me in, for the parents He'd chosen for me, for the sister I'd gained through another adoption process, and for my husband and children. I sought to reassure her that God had selected my parents and my forever family.

When I hung up the phone, I felt overwhelmed, thinking of all God had done to bring peace to a mother's desperate heart. Now I knew His purpose for the strange blessing my parents gave me in the parking lot that day. It was never about me. It was all about her and her heart.

Through it all, God taught me to look for His involvement in every aspect of our lives, even to the point of honoring the request of my mother, who'd asked for Christian parents for me.

Since I had no words, I retrieved my Bible and began searching for God's own words with which to praise Him. I thought I would land in the Psalms, but God had a different word for me.

Whoever obeys his [the king's] command will come to no harm, and the wise heart will know the proper time and procedure. For there is a proper time and procedure for every matter, though a person may be weighed down by misery. (Ecclesiastes 8:5–6 NIV)

A couple of months later, my husband and I made a day trip to meet Mrs. Nancy and her husband, Tom, at their home. (No information was given about my birthfather. The siblings were scheduled to arrive a little later. Tom invited us in, asked us to have a seat on the couch, and then he rolled Mrs. Nancy in her wheelchair from the bedroom into the living room. I'll never forget the look on her face when she saw me. She kept repeating, "You're so beautiful. You're so beautiful."

I gave her a photo album filled with as much of my life as I could put together, along with a double picture frame. On one side I'd placed a picture of me at the age of five and half months, just after my adoption. The other side held a more recent photo of myself. Each picture in the album mesmerized her. Tom turned the pages, encouraging her to move on to the next and the next. She stared intently at each picture, gazing into a life she had been separated from.

When she was done, she told me her story and how she'd arrived at the decision to let me go. Out of respect for her privacy, I will not share her story here. It is hers to tell, not mine.

After a couple of hours visiting with Mrs. Nancy and her husband, it was time to meet my siblings. All four were next door at my sister Terri's home, waiting for the call to come over. As soon as they hit the back door, cameras flashed and hugs came at us from all directions. I felt as if I was having an out-of-body experience, watching a slow-motion reunion of long-lost siblings on *The Oprah Winfrey Show*.

I believe my favorite comment of the afternoon was from my only brother as he referred to something I wrote in a birthday card I'd sent him a month earlier: "I always dreamed of having an older brother. I can't wait to meet you."

With tears in his eyes, he said, "I'm sure I'm not the brother you always dreamed of, but here I am."

Yep. He was right. I never imagined a skinny, scruffy, straight-up ol' country boy wearing blue jeans, a white T-shirt, and pointy cowboy boots all tucked underneath a snakeskin-wrapped cowboy hat. (Now I know where this boots- and jeans-lovin' girl gets it. It's in my DNA. And to further prove it, for over twenty years, my best friend called me "Barn Girl.") He then leaned in and gave me the biggest, sweetest brotherly hug ever.

Soon we left for dinner. Because my birthmother was not able to leave the house, she and her husband stayed home. Jimmy told us he'd won the King Redneck of South Carolina contest for the past five years. He kept us laughing through the entire meal. Everyone seemed glad Rick and I had come.

Before we left the restaurant to drive home, my newfound siblings gave me a gift and a card. Inside the gift bag I found a little light-brown, stuffed bear cub with the words "Cub #5" written on the tag. Macy explained that Tom, Mrs. Nancy's husband, had always referred to them as his bear cubs, and they wanted to add me to the "den." I will always cherish the sweet gesture, the cub, the card, and the thoughtfulness of these new friends.

What a day it was—one that taught me much about God's kindness, love, and forgiveness. I did see my birthmother one more time but chose not to develop an ongoing relationship. Two of the sisters came to visit me, to meet my mom, and to watch my daughter's cheer competition. Since then, I've seen Macy several times, and she has written an article for my magazine. We discovered early that we both love crafting words for others to read.

Had I not responded to God's prompting, I would have missed the unexpected pleasure of God using me to bring peace and healing to a mother's broken heart. Forgiveness truly is the key to unlocking imprisoned hearts and unleashing God's matchless joy.

***

> God is light and in Him there is no darkness at all (1 John 1:5b NASB)

No matter where you are on this salvation journey, God is there, even in your darkest hours. He will never leave you nor forsake you (Hebrews 13:5).

Remember these truths:

- You have a Wonderful Counselor ready to listen and to direct your steps.

- You have a Redeemer making all things beautiful, even your brokenness.

- You have a Savior ready to forgive and wipe your sins from His memory.

- You have a Physician who can heal you from your past, remove your shame and guilt, and move you forward for His purpose and glory.

You are never alone. I encourage you to seek His face each day, listening for His voice. Take hold of His hand and walk by faith in the power of the Holy Spirit. He's waiting to unlock your heart and unleash your joy. If you belong to Christ, you already have access to the key, so use it today.

***

Prepare to share how God has worked in your heart over the past eight weeks. What have you learned about your own heart's condition? Ask your small group or a group of friends to pray about them as you seek to obey what God has shown you. End this session in a time of prayer. If you're part of a larger group setting, your leader may ask you to break into smaller groups and pray for each other. As you finish, make a commitment to continue to pray for one another.

*Birth family names have been changed.

_____

_____

_____

_____

_____

_____

_____

_____

_____

_____

_____

_____

_____

_____

_____

_____

"Getting over a painful experience is much like crossing monkey bars. You have to let go at some point in order to move forward."

~ C.S. Lewis

Afterword

Joy. This theme bombards our culture today. You can find joy just about anywhere—on coffee mugs, magazine covers, T-shirts, and jewelry. I even have a wooden spoon with the word carved into it. Books have been written about it, Bible studies have examined it, devotionals focus on it. Someone, somewhere is always talking about, and looking for, joy.

What is joy?

Some of you are already thinking of the acronym Jesus, Others, You. Though that is a simplified, memorable version of the gospel, joy goes way beyond an acronym. Joy is a deep-rooted confidence in Jesus Christ. Joy is knowing that, no matter what happens, everything will be okay. It's not a cliché. A life built on the firm foundation of Jesus Christ will not be shaken. We are more than conquerors. Doesn't that speak joy to you? It certainly does to me.

First Peter chapter one reveals the root of joy. Verses 5–9 make me want to shout it from the rooftops:

> You are being guarded by God's power through faith for a salvation that is ready to be revealed in the last time. You rejoice in this, even though now for a short time, if necessary, you suffer grief in various trials so that the proven character of your faith—more valuable than gold which, though perishable, is refined by fire—may result in praise, glory, and honor at the revelation

of Jesus Christ. Though you have not seen him, you love him; though not seeing him now, you believe in him, and you rejoice with inexpressible and glorious joy, because you are receiving the goal of your faith, the salvation of your souls. [CSB]

Walking by faith moves us toward the goal of our faith: the salvation of our souls. That is what joy is all about. We have unwavering confidence in Jesus Christ to complete the redemptive work He began in us. This undeniable truth brings joy to life.

Joy is trust.

Joy is faith.

Joy is hope.

Joy is peace.

Joy is Jesus.

Completing *Unlocked Hearts, Unleashed Joy: Forgiveness Is the Key* will not bring you joy. Your response to God will determine whether or not you move toward the goal of your faith with the joy of Christ deep in your soul.

Backstory

In 2005, after spending most of her life ministering through music, Melanie Shull began to pray for God to expand her borders of influence for Him. Through reading His Word and praying, she knew God wanted her to leave a singing group she had belonged to for many years. She had often shared her personal story of adoption and connected it with God's redemptive story of spiritual adoption, but now she sensed God calling her to write it as well.

In 2007, Melanie attended her first Christian writers' conference. She says, "The only thing I knew when I arrived was that I had come to hear specific direction from God. I needed to know how He wanted me to honor Him with this newfound desire to write."

For the entire weekend, Melanie tuned her heart to the voice of the Holy Spirit, knowing He would lead her.

On the last day of the conference, she still had not received clear direction. But as she loaded her luggage into her car to return home, a still, small voice spoke these words into her heart: *You are going to start a magazine, and you're going to call it Living Real ~ Real Life. Real Faith. Real People.*

Because of her faith, obedience, and availability to the Holy Spirit, Melanie's prayers were answered far beyond anything she could have imagined.

But she knew nothing about writing, much less publishing a magazine. She had no clue where to begin. Although the task seemed daunting, she received the challenge with great enthusiasm. All the way home she sang and offered praise to Jesus. She had her answer, and she knew He would bring it to fruition.

Soon God revealed that He had been orchestrating this call for years, through His networking of people already involved in her life: designers, printers, sponsors, and writers. He had gone before her, setting the groundwork for every detail. Because of her lack of knowledge, skills, or experience, Melanie takes none of the credit. All glory goes to Christ because *Living Real* was His idea.

In October of 2009, *Living Real Magazine* hit the streets. Five thousand copies were printed and distributed throughout the midlands of South Carolina. Today, God continues to affirm His call on Melanie's life, expanding her borders of influence through *Living Real Magazine* (adapted from www.livingrealmag.com).

Leader Guide

Suggestions to Enhance Your Small-Group Experience

Thank you for your willingness to lead. You have stepped into a rewarding role, a great responsibility many are unwilling to accept, and for that I am grateful. I have prayed for God to move among all the leaders, asking Him to multiply your time as you pray, prepare, and spend time in the Word. I've asked Him to give each leader an open mind and a willing heart to deal with any issues the Holy Spirit reveals. I've also prayed for strong, healthy friendships within each group. Strong relationships lead to transparency in discussions. I hope the relationships formed here will continue through the weeks, months, and years to come.

I've intentionally not divided this study into weeks but rather lessons, offering you the freedom to move at the pace that best benefits the group.

The following are some strategies I use to boost enthusiasm and participation in my small groups.

Provide a Safe and Welcoming Atmosphere

Make sure the meeting place is clean, calming, and comfortable. I burn a lightly scented candle or put essential oils in a diffuser. Greet the women as they come through the door, or designate a greeter. Serve refreshments or a light meal at each gathering. Food naturally enhances the fellowship time before the study time. Invite the women to sign up to bring refreshments. If you have a large group, encourage several to sign up for each week.

Make sure your meeting space is a safe place for them to talk, bear one another's burdens, and feel loved just as they are. Remind them that everything said here is confidential. This is vital to developing trust.

During your first gathering, allow time for the women to introduce themselves to the group, share a little about themselves, and tell why they chose to participate in this study.

For a more creative introduction, have each participant write their name and three of their favorite things on a piece of paper and place them in a basket or bowl. Take turns drawing the papers from the bowl. Read the list of favorite things and let the ladies guess who wrote it. This fun activity helps the ladies begin learning something about each other at the first session.

Always Begin and End Your Time with Prayer

Spend quality time in prayer for and with one another. This may mean breaking into groups of twos or threes, depending on the size of the group. Identify prayer-group leaders beforehand so you can speak to them in advance and make sure they are willing to lead prayer. If your group is small, you may want to lead the prayer time yourself if no one volunteers to pray.

Collect Contact Information

Have a notebook or kiosk at the door. Nametags are always helpful.

If you have an advance sign-up, get their information then. You may want to send a note, the agenda, and/or some instructions ahead of time.

Let's SWAP (Sisters with a Purpose)

SWAP is a helpful tool I designed to keep the women motivated and connected. There are several ways to SWAP (and you may think of others).

Every week, ask each woman to write her address on an envelope. Alternately, let them fill out all six at one time. Collect the envelopes. At the end of each lesson, ask the participants to select one envelope, making sure they don't draw their own, and keep the person's identity secret. Hand out blank notecards that match the envelopes (the cuter the better). Ask each person to write a short note of encouragement to the woman they selected. The reveal occurs when they receive the card in the mail.

Handwritten notes are becoming a lost art, but receiving a personal note through the mail is priceless. A genuine handwritten note lets the person know you are thinking about them and praying for them between sessions. You can choose to have them write the notes before they leave, and you can mail them. Or let them take the envelope and card with them and mail it themselves before the next gathering. If someone is absent, then the leader will write a note. Only those in attendance participate in the SWAP for that week.

Alternately, each woman may send notes throughout the course of the study, like a secret sister. Each woman would sign her card, "Your SWAP Sister." At the last gathering, prepare to celebrate what God has done through the study and then reveal the secret SWAPs. You may have a small gift exchange to make it even more fun. Gifts could reflect something they've learned about the person over the course of the study, or it may be an item from their favorite-things list from week one. The point is to have fun!

Encourage Table Talk

This works best in a large-group setting. If your space allows, set up tables (round tables work best) for natural grouping to take place. During the discussion times, give the groups a few minutes to talk among themselves about what they've learned during the week and to answer the questions.

Always Be Prepared

Each week, make sure you have worked and prayed through the material, are familiar with the subject matter, and can lead the discussion questions. Use other reliable resources, such as commentaries, other Bible versions, a concordance, or other leaders or teachers as necessary. If questions arise that you cannot answer or don't feel comfortable with, be honest and say so. Our love for studying the Word of God will motivate our participants to fall in love with His Word as well. Remember, the Holy Spirit is the teacher, and we must learn to trust Him with His role, and to seek out wise counsel to help us learn.

Host an Author Meet and Greet

I would love to meet you. Scheduling a Facetime meeting or inviting an author to come and speak to your Bible study group, book club, or women's event, always enhances the reader's experience. If you would be interested in connecting with me, please contact me at hello@livingrealmag.com. Nothing brings me more pleasure than hearing from people who have discovered, or who would like to discover, that forgiveness is the key to unlocking hearts and unleashing joy.

Order Information

REDEMPTION PRESS

To order additional copies of this book, please visit
www.redemption-press.com.
Also available on Amazon.com and BarnesandNoble.com
Or by calling toll free 1-844-2REDEEM.

CPSIA information can be obtained
at www.ICGtesting.com
Printed in the USA
FSHW020747170519

9 781683 147732